CW00502233

HOW TO BE VISIBLE WITH SOCIAL MEDIA

BUSINESS SKILLS FOR EDITORS: 3

Louise Harnby

Copyright © 2020 Louise Harnby

The right of Louise Harnby to be identified as the author of this work has been asserted by her in accordance with the Copyright, Designs and Patents Act 1988. All rights reserved. This book is sold subject to the condition that it shall not, by way of trade or otherwise, be lent, re-sold, hired out or otherwise circulated in any form of binding or cover other than that in which it is published and without a similar condition including this condition being imposed on the subsequent purchaser.

ISBN: 9798667557029

CONTENTS

1. Introduction

Overview

There's a difference between using social media and having a social media strategy. A strategy is what we're focusing on – purposeful social media activity that makes us visible and compelling.

Using social media will get us so far. It will enable us to connect with people in our editorial and wider publishing network ... and have a lot of fun with friends and family.

A *strategy*, however, puts us top of mind so that we're visible beyond social media. Our skills, knowledge, experience, blogs, vlogs, podcasts, training courses, speaking engagements, conferences and websites become visible too, not just in people's minds but also in the search engines.

Paying for promotion

I believe that editorial business owners can achieve a huge amount on social media without spending a bean. That's what this guide focuses on.

However, there are paid-for options: Twitter ads, Facebook ads and post boosts, and LinkedIn ads. So should you pay?

If you think it might help you to achieve your goals, then by all means carry out a test. For example, you could pay a few pounds or dollars to boost a well-performing post on your Facebook Page. If your goal is to generate new leads, and you're successful, great.

Even if you don't achieve the goal it's not a failure. You've learned something valuable: that you should invest your marketing cash elsewhere.

It's worth commissioning a social media professional if you're thinking about spending money on social media. For example, to get the best out of Facebook ads, you'll need to have installed a pixel on your website. If you're not sure what that is, or why it's important, it's time to call in the pros.

'But my clients aren't on social media'

If you think social media is an empty nest when it comes to your clients, think again.

First, are you absolutely sure? Have you checked? These days, it's unusual for businesses not to use social media. As for individual clients, often we don't know who they are so how can we know where they are?

Even if they're not using it to find help, they might check out your social media profiles to verify that you're real, to evaluate your experience and assess your suitability, and to see whether you know how to behave yourself on public platforms. A well-presented social media profile can therefore act as social proof.

If your clients aren't using social media as a search engine now, might they do so further down the line? Futureproof your business – today's clients might not be tomorrow's. Think longer term rather than in the bubble of now.

Even if your clients aren't and never will use social media, your colleagues are using it; they talk about you, share your advice and resources, even recommend you to their clients. They are your advocates. Advocates are like human search engines (consider the questions people ask in social media forums and groups, the results generated, and the names mentioned).

Resources

Most of the resources I've linked to are free. Some of you might be at the start of your client-acquisition journey; those of you with mature businesses might still have financial commitments that eat into your earnings and make business-investment decisions challenging. Editorial work isn't always as well-paying as some would like, particularly when we're building visibility, and I recognize this.

Some of the resources do have paid-for options with increased functionality. Do you need them? I don't believe so. When you're comfortable with the management of your purposeful social media marketing, by all means give the trial paid-for versions a go and evaluate whether the productivity gains are worth the investment.

2. Emotion and mechanics

Overview

Most working definitions of social media offer something on the lines of the following:

> Internet-based communication tools that allow people to connect, deliver and consume information.

That's all very well, but it misses something critical: it focuses on the mechanical. That's no longer enough. To stand out and get attention, we need to embrace emotion. There's too much noisy traffic on social media to ignore it.

- Social = *emotional*: it's about connection, interaction, engagement, relationships
- Media = *mechanical*: it's an instrument of communication

It's only when we use these instruments of communication to make people feel something that we can begin to be heard.

Emotion is key because it makes our marketing **sticky**. By this, I mean that people feel compelled to continue engaging with us long after we've posted, shared, commented, blogged, vlogged, and tweeted. They won't always remember exactly what we did, what we posted or what we wrote, but they will remember how we made them feel.

An online world in flux

Most of us are aware of Facebook, LinkedIn, and Twitter. The online world is constantly in flux though. As platforms introduce new ways of engaging, so the parameters of what constitutes social media change.

For example, YouTube is not just a place to host videos. It's a search engine and a space in which to have conversations, to share, to engage. It's a searchable community in which you can invite people to follow your channel. And given the power of video in social media marketing, YouTube can't be ignored when we're thinking about purposefulness.

And how about a blog? Or Facebook Messenger, Google Hangouts and Behance? If they allow connection, delivery and consumption, might we also consider them social media?

In this day and age, it's best if we keep an open mind and focus on our audience and the opportunity to engage rather than on what we think counts as social media.

Why you should use social media

Marketing and communication have changed. The internet is democratic. Those with the biggest advertising budgets are not the only winners; those with the most engagement can join in the fun, too.

Social media platforms act as conduits for **engagement** and **relationship building**. Like the search engines, they reward engagement. That means that even the little guys like you and me can have big wins: visibility and business growth.

Through social media we can:

- have conversations with colleagues and clients
- ask questions and provide answers
- upload recorded video and audio
- upload branded images
- go live with video and audio
- post blog articles in their entirety
- share links to valuable, educational content
- deliver resources (books, tip sheets, checklists)
- curate content (our own and others')
- generate website traffic

Caution: Just because you can doesn't mean you should. See Appendix 2 for some ideas about how *not* to get in a pickle!

The emotions you arouse

Think about the emotions you want to arouse in your network of colleagues and clients. What would you like them to say about you when you're not in the room?

Here are a few examples.

- He makes me feel happy – he's always kind, supportive and respectful
- He makes me feel focused – he gives me the tools to achieve my goals
- He makes me feel in control – he gives me resources that save me time
- He makes me feel excited – like there's light at the end of the tunnel
- She makes me feel skilled – she educates me with her tutorials
- She makes me feel included – I'm part of a bigger community
- She makes me feel relieved – she offers solutions to my problems
- She makes me feel confident – she shows me how to move forward when I feel like I'm drowning

For you to do ...

- Create a strategy workbook to record your decisions.
- Record the emotions you'd like to arouse in your audience.

3. Understanding the algorithms

Overview

Here's something every editorial professional needs to know in order to get the very best from social media: All social media platforms want us to stay on their land (whereas we want to guide people to our land, e.g. our website).

To understand why, we need to consider the algorithms – their purpose and their impact.

What the algorithms do and why

Essentially, platforms are noisy. Millions use them. To keep people engaged (and enhance the user experience), a platform needs to work out a way of prioritizing what appears in people's feeds. The **algorithm** is the answer.

Every social media platform has an algorithm. It measures what's popular and interesting, for example by likes, shares, clicks, saves, comments, and time spent watching a video.

And once it knows what it thinks interests you – what arouses emotion in you – it pushes that in your face. Why? Partly it's about **engagement** (you'll continue to find the platform interesting and use it to communicate) and partly (well, mainly) it's about **money**.

Engagement – the friendly neighbour

Imagine you live at 11 Facebook Street. You invite friends and family to your home to celebrate your dad's birthday. Everyone's grateful to you for hosting the event. Lots of people talk about how you've put on a great party – on this occasion and in the past. All well and good.

Then a neighbour turns up and puts a sign up in your front garden: ALTERNATIVE PARTY VENUE AT 13 WEBSITE STREET. You're nice so you don't object. But when another neighbour turns up with a sign that says THE BEST PARTIES ARE AT 11 FACEBOOK STREET, you give him a pat on the back and direct everyone's attention to his sign. He's neighbourly.

Friendly neighbours create pleasant community spaces that people recommend and choose to return to. Social media recognizes this and rewards neighbourly behaviour.

Money, money, money!

Of course, social media platforms are not just rewarding the friendliest people. There's money at stake, too. Lots of it.

Let's look at Facebook. Click on the Home tab in the top blue ribbon. In that feed you'll see not only your network members' posts but also a whole load of sponsored stuff (from people you don't know but who paid to boost their posts). And on the right-hand side of the stream are the paid-for advertisements.

In Facebook's eyes, the longer we stay on its turf, the more likely we are to see one of those promotions and click on it. And if the advertisers earn money from their investment, they'll continue to buy these services from Facebook. So when we post content that keeps others on its land, Facebook gives us another pat on the back.

Trumping the cute puppies

What kind of content keeps people on social media? What do we engage with, feel emotional about? All of the following: fun pictures of our kids doing something hilarious, videos of cute puppies oozing gorgeousness, holiday snaps, dramatic events, and shocking news.

All of that content is engaging and consumable. We hit the like, love, anger, or wow buttons to show our appreciation, adoration, fury, or amazement. We express those emotions through comments, too. And so we should. There's nothing wrong with that. But there's a huge amount of content that falls into those categories, especially the cute and funny stuff.

As business owners using social media purposefully, we have to compete with the cute puppies for people's interest and engagement, otherwise we might as well not bother using it as a business tool.

That means acknowledging how the algorithms work and playing the game to our own advantage (and the advantage of our clients and colleagues).

More top tips on social media algorithms

At the time of writing, this is the state of play.

- New posts are shown more than older posts; it's therefore worth posting regularly to show your network that you're an engaged professional.
- Aim to build a relevant audience. Non-editors and non-potential clients (like your mum or your best friend!) won't engage with your business posts meaningfully. Having a family network the size of the Waltons won't help you achieve your goals. Grandma won't ask your ManyChat bot to deliver a proofreading checklist, won't read your LinkedIn article about the different levels of editing, and won't share your tweet about how to punctuate dialogue … because she's not interested (unless she's an editor or a writer). It's quality not quantity all the way.
- Make sure your business posts are relevant to your intended audience. Like it or not, social media platforms know a lot about you and your network so they will prioritize the posts in your networks' newsfeeds that they think will be of most interest to those people. See the chapter on holism – networking, posting, and content creation are not distinct activities; they're connected.
- Focus on providing value. When ranking your posts, the algorithms don't just look at current performance but past performance too. Thus, a high-value post today – with lots of clicks, retweets, shares, or comments – will positively affect a post tomorrow. Of course, the flip side is that a low-performing post today will negatively affect the ranking of tomorrow's post. Lesson: keep the quality of your offering high at all times.
- Social media platforms are more likely to show you the kinds of media that you respond to. So if you tend to click on gifs on Twitter, Twitter will prioritize that kind of

content in your feed. And, of course, the same applies to your followers. Purposeful social media engagement therefore requires us to post content in the format that our target users prefer. It's always about your audience's preferences, not your own.

- Some platforms' algorithms reward you for having a complete profile. Complete profiles indicate authenticity. If you receive notifications (e.g. from LinkedIn) telling you that your profile is not yet complete, pay attention.

4. Being purposeful with social media

Overview

Whose house do you work in? Purposeful social media engagement is relevant to freelance *and* in-house editors. I'm an independent editorial business owner and my strategy is pertinent to fellow independent editorial pros (for example, editors, proofreaders, indexers, translators, copywriters). But if you work in-house, and even if your employer isn't a sponsor, you can still use social media to achieve the following:

- Make yourself a visible, discoverable editor
- Present yourself as a thought leader
- Demonstrate your engagement with the industry beyond your office cubicle

Do you have a time machine?

Those of us without a TARDIS or a DeLorean don't know what's around the corner. Will you be in-house forever? What will you be doing in five years' time?

- Still in-house in the same role?
- Still in-house in a more senior role?
- Still in-house but head of social media marketing?
- Freelance but still working for publishers?
- Freelance but working for new publishers?
- Freelance but working for independent writers?

For 13 years I worked happily for two international publishing companies – first for Williams & Wilkins, later for SAGE Publishing. Until I had a child I'd never considered going it alone but as of 2017 I've been running my own business, from my own house, for over a decade. When I first went out on my own, all my work was with publishers. I didn't need to be visible on Google or

LinkedIn to get work. But now I edit solely for indie authors – I didn't see that coming 10 years ago but visibility is everything to me now. And social media is part of that mix.

Every professional, wherever they work, whatever building they live in, can use social media to demonstrate their expertise, engagement, and connection with the editorial, publishing, language, and writing communities. And in so doing, they can build their audience, reinforce their brand, and expand their visibility. Using social media purposefully is therefore a means of **future proofing**.

What are your intentions?

Social media is great for chattering – updates about our kids' first day back at school, little notes about how badly we need coffee, pictures of our cats sitting on our keyboards. It's all great fun and long may it continue. But when it comes to using social media for business, we need to think about purpose. Otherwise the dreaded rabbit hole will beckon.

Purposeful social media usage means doing something to achieve something else.

Here are a few examples.

Do this	Achieves this
Upload a native blog post to LinkedIn about a training course you're running.	Increases awareness and encourage course sales.
Create a Facebook Messenger bot campaign that delivers a self-proofreading resource.	Expands audience reach. Engages with fellow proofreaders and writer clients. Demonstrates experience and knowledge. Encourages signup to blog and service commission.
Tweet a linked statement about a PDF on editing crime fiction. Include a gif.	The gif makes the tweet stand out. The PDF demonstrates expertise and encourages clients to visit your website and hire your editing services.

Pose a business question on your LinkedIn timeline. Tag colleagues who might have an interesting opinion.	The responses can be used to generate a research-based blog post or a booklet.
Share a colleague's blog post on Twitter and Facebook Page.	Demonstrates that you're an engaged reciprocator.
Engage with a client's tweet.	Your client is followed by others who might also need your services so you're expanding your reach.
Create and post an image or infographic that summarizes a key business learning point.	Demonstrates knowledge. Provides clients and colleagues with something eye-catching in the noise of social media that might drive them to your website for more information.
Offer solutions to problems posed by colleagues or clients in core Facebook groups.	Shows off your specialisms. Demonstrates your engagement and professionalism. Leads to work referrals, requests to contribute guest blog posts, vlogs, and podcasts. Creates training and presenting opportunities.
Post a video natively to Facebook about your services or a resource you've written.	Expands audience reach. Allows colleagues and clients to see the real you. Offers alternative delivery platform for written content.

Purposeful social media usage **isn't** about the following:

- Whining
- Ranting
- Exposing our weaknesses or failures (or others' for that matter!)

Every minute we spend on the above is a minute we could be doing the following instead:

- Building awareness about our skills and services
- Learning about new tools, approaches, and viewpoints
- Engaging positively with colleagues and clients – building relationships
- Solving other people's problems
- Solving our own problems
- Increasing our business's visibility
- Encouraging traffic to our websites
- Generating opportunities for paid work (training, speaking, writing, editing)

Case study – moving outside your bubble

When I post on social media, one of my intentions is to get the attention of people outside my network who might drive my business forward in some way. Through this they might:

- Introduce me to an audience that I'm not yet connected with
- Offer me a promotion opportunity
- Commission my services
- Share my content
- Buy my books or training classes

In 2017 I became aware of Tim Lewis, the host of the Begin Self-Publishing Podcast. Self-publishing authors are my target clients. Tim isn't in my editorial network and we've not yet attended the same conferences. However, I was interested in what he was doing and thought it would be amazing if I had the opportunity to talk about freelance fiction editing on his podcast.

I began to follow him on Twitter, Facebook and LinkedIn. I engaged with him by liking, commenting on, and sharing his excellent posts on all three platforms. Over the course of several months I got his attention. He reciprocated – sharing the content I posted about on social media to his network of self-publishers and marketers.

Then, in August, he messaged me on Facebook and asked if I'd be a guest on his podcast!

The important point is that I didn't ask for this; rather, I earned it. I used social media to show him what I do, what makes me tick and what I'm interested in professionally.

Results

- Podcast interview (September 2017)
- LinkedIn endorsement (October 2017)
- Recommendation to another book-related podcaster (November 2017)
- Audience reach #1: Tim frequently shares my posts on Twitter to his 11.5K followers (four times the size of my own audience)
- Audience reach #2: One of his followers began to follow me too; that person (an author) now retweets my author-related content to his 105K followers

This example demonstrates how intention leads to action, which in turn leads to results.

For you to do …

Think about your own intentions with social media. What do you want to achieve? Examples might include:

- Delivering content
- Connecting with influencers within your colleague network and client networks
- Promoting your products and services
- Advertising a training course
- Expanding your online audience
- Making yourself more visible in the search engines

Use your strategy workbook to record the goals you'd like to achieve through social media engagement.

5. Thinking holistically

Overview

I recommend thinking about social media as part of a bigger whole rather than as a distinct, standalone entity, something to be ticked off a list. All the things that we do as professionals are interconnected. Running a business is like looking at DNA. Actions and behaviour on one point of the chain affect actions and behaviour elsewhere.

Furthermore, it's my belief that when we're performing for others (speaking at conferences, presenting ideas in a focus-group, talking during company coffee breaks, tweeting business resources, commenting on Facebook posts, posting articles on LinkedIn, adding images to a Pinterest board, uploading a video to YouTube) we are **marketing**. This applies no matter whose house we work in.

Social media and general marketing

Marketing is about selling ourselves as professionals so that others want to engage with us and buy from us. It's why editors don't turn up at the ACES annual conference or the London Book Fair wearing bikinis and wellington boots. It's why we don't insult colleagues on Twitter or post pictures of ourselves in our underwear on our Facebook Page. Social media is therefore part of our marketing strategy when we use it purposefully.

Even if we think we're just having a chat with colleagues in a closed Facebook group about how many passes we carry out during a line edit or contributing to a conference call with in-house production editors, we're still marketing ourselves.

Reputations can be built and busted on social media. And that's why we shouldn't do any of the things listed in Appendix 2.

Holism in action – a fictive case study

The case study featuring my engagement with Tim Lewis demonstrates the interconnectedness social media – how actions in one place deliver business-promotion opportunities, audience reach, endorsements and recommendations in another. Here's a second example; this one's made up.

You regularly offer solutions to problems in one large Facebook editorial forum. That's made you visible to a large network of colleagues. They are your advocates. You also host a blog that publishes content aimed at your clients – writing tools, novel craft, editor selection, dealing with writers' block, self-publishing problems, how to find an agent, etc. You use several core social media platforms as a stage on which to promote, link to, and deliver this content. Your advocate colleagues think it's useful stuff too (for their clients and for them).

- They share your posts in other online communities, which means more people become aware of you and what you're doing.
- They connect with you and visit your website. That's expanded audience reach.
- They visit your blog and sign up for your mailing list. That's increased awareness.
- Not all editors are the same. We have different skill sets. Some – the oranges – specialize in sentence-level work, while others – the apples – are developmentally focused. When clients ask oranges for developmental editing, they refer these people to the apples. In this example, you're an apple so that's an increase in work leads.
- ACES hears that you're creating content and offering solutions online. They offer to pay you to run a class in developmental editing. That's expanded audience reach, a new training skillset, a boost to your reputation, and additional income.

- Knowledge about that course leads to more visitors to your website, more signups to your blog, more links to your content, more visibility in the search engines, and more clients contacting you. You decide to increase your prices because you're never short of work. That's more income for no additional effort.

This is one example of how purposeful social media engagement is bound up with visibility, SEO, content, perceived professionalism, business development opportunities, and your income stream.

We must ensure we don't fall into the trap of placing different business activities (e.g. marketing, networking, speaking) into distinct compartments. And even if we prefer to visualize our business in this way, we must acknowledge that the walls are permeable.

Social media and SEO – in brief

What counts today might not count tomorrow. The algorithms change often, precisely because the search engines and social media platforms know there will always be those who try to game the system maliciously rather than work with it purposefully.

Here are a few tips:

- The number of followers you have on Twitter and the number of likes you have on Facebook are not relevant to Google (at the moment) but are relevant to Bing (still a big search engine).
- Links to your social media content – Twitter, LinkedIn, Facebook, and YouTube – are relevant to the search engines. Links provide credibility and determine who's ranked and where.
- Social media profiles show up in the search engines.
- Social media channels are search engines in themselves. Your clients and colleagues might do keyword searches to

find answers to problems or to look for specific service providers (e.g. #proofreader on Twitter).

6. Social media and content marketing

Overview

Essentially, content marketing is about value – creating and delivering useful and usually free stuff. People are grateful and they remember you. They talk about your content, link to it, and share it. Google uses that as an indicator of your interestingness. The upshot is that you become more visible to people and to the search engines.

Used purposefully, social media is critical to a content marketing strategy because:

- it facilitates sharing
- it facilitates delivery (links, native hosting, and onsite delivery via chatbots)
- it provides a stage on which to place images and text that are visible to your network (native uploads)
- it can generate traffic to your website

What content?

You can either upload content natively or link to material that you've placed elsewhere. For example, you might upload a video tutorial natively to Facebook, or embed a link to an article on your website that in turn links to a video on a third-party platform such as YouTube, Twitter or LinkedIn. Consider the following:

- Blog posts, vlog content and podcast episodes
- Booklets and tip sheets
- Tutorials
- Event news (your training courses and speaking engagements)

By 'natively' I mean that you physically upload the content to a social media platform rather than linking to a third-party site (e.g. your website, YouTube or Vimeo).

Here are some case studies of content marketing and social media in action.

Case study 1

I created a booklet for self-publishing authors (my target client group): *The Author's Proofreading Companion*. It provides independent writers with guidance on how to tidy up a Word document.

It's free content and its purpose is to make authors think that I'm helpful, kind, knowledgeable and experienced. I hope they'll feel more inclined to hire me.

Because it's useful, authors and colleagues are more likely to talk about it, link to it, and share it. Google likes that and rewards me for my interestingness with higher rankings.

This strategy will only work if people know about the booklet. This is where social media is my content marketing delivery hero. Here's what I did:

Social media delivery

- LinkedIn and Twitter added to social media rotation schedules
- Facebook Profile: promoted once (viewable by my existing audience)
- Facebook Page: promoted via a chatbot trigger-word campaign on my Page once (viewable to my existing audience and beyond)
- Image pinned to Pinterest page

Results

- Audience reach on Facebook: 11,589
- Audience reach on website (page views) (Nov 2016–Nov 2017): 2,416

- Downloads direct from Messenger (via Facebook chatbot campaign): 271
- Downloads direct from website (Nov 2016–Nov 2017): 119
- Facebook comments, shares and likes: 371

Note the impact of the chatbot campaign – that one Facebook campaign was twice as powerful in terms of downloads than all the other social media activity that linked back to a download from my website, and nearly five times as powerful in terms of eyes on the resource.

It's proof that when we combine our knowledge of the social media algorithm with our content marketing, we can generate superb engagement.

Case study 2

Editor Denise Cowle repurposes her website's blog posts for LinkedIn every few months.

Social media delivery

In January 2017 she published an article on her website about using profanity in online content, and the degree to which the editor should intervene: 'Expletive deleted – how far do you go?' She followed up by reposting the same article natively on LinkedIn only a day later.

Results

- Website article: 21 Facebook likes and 12 comments
- LinkedIn article: 100 LinkedIn likes and 38 comments

By delivering her content natively on a social media platform, Denise expanded her audience reach well beyond what was possible on her website alone. And given that she specializes in proofreading and copyediting non-fiction, making an impact on a platform with such a strong corporate presence was a great call on her part.

Case study 3

Some of you will already be familiar with Paul Beverley's excellent free editorial macros. Paul began creating video tutorials in 2017 that help his colleagues install and run his macros with no fuss. He uploads these to his YouTube channel.

Paul has 207 YouTube subscribers. He knows that many thousands of editors who are already using (or might like to use) his content are hanging out on Facebook and that most of them aren't yet subscribing to his channel.

He posts links to his videos in relevant Facebook groups in order to grab the attention of his audience.

Social media delivery

One tutorial, 'Wildcarding Techniques 1', was posted in the following groups in November 2017:

- Editors Who Talk Tech
- Editors' Association of Earth
- EAE Backroom

Results

If Paul had uploaded his video to YouTube and left it at that, he'd have limited his audience reach to 207 (his YouTube subscriber base at that time).

By posting his excellent content into relevant groups he reached 8,000+ editors.

Expanding content reach

Content that is **invisible** and **unmovable** is of **no economic value**. Social media turns on the lights and supplies the delivery truck.

When we use social media as part of our content marketing strategy, we get eyes on our resources. And the more people who see it, the more likely we are to receive likes, shares, comments and engagement – all of which helps to make us visible in the search engines and top of our colleagues' and clients' minds.

If you have great content, share it on the social media platforms that your audience is using.

For you to do ...

Think about the types of content you could create for your audience and deliver via social media. How can you solve problems and arouse positive emotions such that you're top of mind for commissions and referrals? Consider the following:

- Checklists and tip sheets
- Articles
- Video tutorials and screencasts
- Reviews of tools, courses and books
- Ebooks and booklets and pamphlets

Use your strategy workbook to record your content plans and how you could use social media to make those resources visible.

7. Searchable content curation

Overview

Social media is searchable. That means your detective clients and colleagues can hunt for stuff! The game is on so put yourself in Sherlock's shoes! Remember, when you're searchable, you're discoverable.

Some social media platforms lend themselves particularly well to content curation, in particular those that have dashboards rather than timeline or newsfeed displays. And if that content is findable through a search, all the better. Two good examples are:

- Pinterest dashboards
- YouTube channels

It's worth bearing in mind that most social media platforms have search functions. If you're posting interesting, useful content onto your core platforms, you're more likely to be found by people outside your network.

- Twitter: Hashtag and keyword searches show results from your feed
- LinkedIn: Keyword searches display relevant service providers
- Facebook: Keyword searches show results from your Page

Why curation pays

Content curation is a great way to make yourself visible on social media:

The algorithms like regular content

We absolutely know this is the case on Facebook because Facebook reminds us when we've neglected our Page. Creating content is time-consuming; curation helps us to keep the platforms happy by using other people's useful content.

The algorithms like a great user experience

Social media platforms want to keep users happy. That means having lots of juicy, useful stuff for them to engage with. When a platform sees that we're helping it achieve its goals, it rewards us by prioritizing our content.

Professional expertise

When we curate others' content, we get to demonstrate our own engagement with our industry but without doing all the work. We also make those followers whose content we're sharing very happy and more likely to reciprocate.

It puts us top of mind in our network

We can make ourselves memorable by being perceived as proactive, generous people who get more eyes on other people's material. That can lead to referrals.

There's a domino effect

Well-performing posts are taken notice of by social media's algorithms. If you share a post from someone in your network and that post is popular, you're seen as someone who provides a great user experience. That impacts on the next post you share – the content is likely to be prioritized higher. If that next post is your own content, you're able to leapfrog on the back of your curated content's high performance. In other words, great curated social media posts make your own posts work harder for you.

For you to do ...

In addition to your own content, who else's might you curate? Consider your target audience and your colleagues. Whose attention do you want to get?

- If you're a proofreader you might curate content created by people with different skills (e.g. a developmental editor).

- If you're a medical editor, you might curate content from the field of medicine and the life sciences.
- If you're an academic editor, you could curate content published by social science scholars.
- If you're a business editor, you could curate marketing and business tips and tools.

Use your strategy workbook to record your curation plans and how you could use social media to make other people's resources visible while presenting yourself as an engaged reciprocator.

8. Which platform? Beware the rabbit hole

Overview

Avoiding the rabbit hole means making some tough decisions about which social media platforms will reward you with the most beneficial engagement. New platforms are constantly emerging, as are ways of using existing ones (e.g. chatbots on Facebook, Twitter's Periscope, Facebook Live, Instagram Stories didn't exist at when those platforms were first launched).

Two rules of thumb

- Be audience-centric – focus on colleagues (who can be advocates, customers and referrers) and clients (who will buy and refer your services). Wherever they are is where you need to be, regardless of your own preferences.
- Don't spread yourself too thin – focus on one or two core platforms and be excellent on those. Trying to work with any more will mean you end up not doing enough, or doing enough but in the rabbit hole.

Facebook, Twitter mainly and LinkedIn are still the three dominant platforms for editorial, writing and publishing folk and offer a powerful suite of tools for sharing, delivering, and consuming multiple types of content.

Within-platform focus

Even within platforms, we need to be selective if we're going to be purposeful. Joining and engaging with colleagues or clients in 20 different Facebook or LinkedIn groups will turn your social media schedule into a catastrophe.

There are numerous groups to choose from – broader business groups of non-editing folk that allow us to view our businesses from beyond an editorial lens; and editorially focused groups that facilitate the discussion of concerns that arise in our day-to-day work.

It's not that there aren't many in which you'd be welcome – there are. It's not that there aren't many you'd enjoy – there are. It's that there are only 24 hours in a day. Each of us must balance the following:

A. The work we do (editing, whether in-house or at home)

B. The work we do to get the work we do (marketing, including the social media aspect)

C. The life we live

- If we do so much of B in a working day that it impacts on our ability to do A, then B has **negative economic value**.
- If we do so much of B in the leisure part of our day that it impacts on our ability to enjoy C, then it has **negative emotional value**.

I recommend picking two or three groups where we learn the most or make the biggest difference. This keeps us disciplined and away from the entrance to the rabbit hole.

Not all groups are free – some are accessible as part of a broader paid-for subscription service. Just because your fee entitles you to access the group doesn't mean you must access it. These need to be evaluated in just the same way because they require your precious time.

Evaluation

- Do you feel welcome – that you're part of a community?
- Do group members help you solve problems?
- Are you able to contribute to solving other members' problems?
- Is the group active such that there are enough members to make discussion meaningful? Are members engaging with you regularly and consistently?
- Do the discussions provide you with ideas for content?

- Do the conversations help you focus your brand message so that you can communicate your fit to potential clients?
- Is membership delivering leads that will generate revenue?
- Are you receiving as much as you give? In other words, is the return on investment of your time sufficient?
- Do you receive feedback when you try something new and challenging?

If the answer to at least three of the above isn't 'yes', consider whether remaining in the group is a purposeful use of your time. If, after several months, any of the following are consistently in play, consider removing yourself and focusing on more productive online venues.

For you to do ...

Which social media platforms will you focus on? Within those platforms, which groups will you choose that will help drive you forward? Remember to consider emotional and economic value, and to be wary of spreading yourself too thin. Ask yourself the following:

- Which platforms are your colleagues and clients using?
- Which groups offer you the most benefits?
- Which groups do you need to evaluate and consider leaving?

Record your platform and group preferences in your strategy workbook.

9. How to get Facebook engagement for free

Overview

Facebook is a superb social media platform for professional editors, especially for connecting with fellow editors and writers. Let's look at how to use it effectively.

The difference between a Page and a Profile

Here's the most important thing you need to know about crafting a strong, purposeful presence on Facebook: there is power in the Page. That's because only via your Page can you get eyes on your posts from beyond your existing network.

If you don't yet have a Facebook Page, then build one. It's the voice of your business, and a very different animal from your personal Profile. Remember, it allows you to get eyes on your content outside your network. The following table summarizes the key differences between a Page and a Profile.

Facebook Page	Facebook Profile
This is your professional Facebook account. It represents you as a business owner. It should curate business news, valuable resources, stories relevant to your industry, business videos and pictures, and showcase your content.	This is your personal Facebook account. It represents you as an individual and will feature information such as life events, stories, status updates, and news. This is where you post your pictures of cute puppies and silly wigs. You can post business news here too if you wish, though not an advert.
Public by default. Anyone can see, like, and follow your Page. It allows you to connect with other individuals and businesses whom you'd rather keep separate from your personal Profile.	Privacy settings are available. People must ask to be your friend and you must accept them.

Those who elect to like and follow you will see your Page posts in their newsfeed (via the Home button).	Your privacy settings will determine who sees your Profile posts in their newsfeed (via the Home button).
Through the Insights tab you can see how well individual posts are performing (metrics such as organic reach, audience demographics, engagement, etc.).	No metrics.
For commercial use – you're allowed to carry out monetized promotions via your Page (ads and boosts).	For non-commercial use. Monetized promotion is a violation of Facebook's terms and conditions.

Most editors are still not using their Facebook Pages consistently and regularly to generate awareness about their businesses, choosing instead to focus on their existing networks via their Profiles. That's a missed opportunity.

Have you received the Facebook notification telling you that you haven't posted on your Page for a while? I received one after not posting for only a few days. Take notice of it – it's telling you something: Facebook thinks Page posts are important; it means that regular posting there is something the algorithm pays attention to. See 'Searchable content curation' for how by posting regularly I've increased the likes on my Page by 63% in 11 months.

Think back to 'Understanding the algorithms', where we discussed how social media platforms reward you for creating engaging content. Your Page is the place to take action.

- If you find an article relevant to your colleagues and clients, post it on your Page.
- If you write a blog post, share it on your Page.
- If you create a useful resource, announce it on your Page.
- If you have news to share about your business, tell people via your Page.
- Discovered a great training course? Share a link or review on your Page.

- Celebrating an industry-related event (e.g. World Book Day)? Mention it on your Page.

To reiterate, it's not that this information can't go on your Profile but rather that your Page is where you'll be able to get eyes on it that are outside your existing network.

If you're not using your Page, you're not maximizing Facebook's free opportunity to demonstrate your expertise and deliver your content to as many people as possible.

Basic premise of engagement

Here's where we focus on how to get that all important boost whereby Facebook puts your post in front of more people (including those who don't follow you) as a reward.

Likes and shares will get you a little push but the biggies are native video (not an embedded link to, for example, YouTube) and comments. It takes longer to watch a video or comment on a post than to click a like button. Facebook figures that watchers and commenters are more interested, and because they're sticking around for longer, they're more likely to see the ads. So when Facebook sees watching and commenting on a Page, it boosts the content.

Offer something valuable (e.g. a tool, a resource, a review); it doesn't matter what tactics you use to increase engagement if what you're offering is worthless.

Ultimately, the numbers aren't important. What counts is that you're making yourself worthy of being visible because you're providing something that helps people. It's like when someone decides they want to build friendships – it's not the numbers they're interested in but what you can all do for each other. That's where the meaningfulness (or in the case of business, purposefulness) lies.

Encouraging commenting

Asking questions is great, but a new and effective way to encourage commenting is to ask for it in exchange for something valuable. As of writing, chatbots are big news. Will this be the case in a year's time? Who knows – that's why I'm doing it now.

Through ManyChat I created a chatbot called Lulu. Lulu allows me to deliver a resource instantly to a commenter via Facebook Messenger. Instead of telling people that I have a free resource for them that's accessible via my website, and then creating a link that takes them off Facebook, Lulu delivers the resource on Facebook's turf.

Everyone's happy – Facebook because people stay on the platform for a little longer; me because lots of people have accessed two resources that I've created for them (no point in wasting my time making them if no one knows they exist); and colleagues and potential clients because they've received something useful.

Some people worry that using chatbots is spammy. It doesn't have to be. Keep it sticky – engage with those who use the bot, give something useful, and chat directly when things so wrong ... and when things go right!

Encouraging attention

One of the best ways of encouraging attention is with video, especially native video.

Love it or loathe it, video is here to stay. Most people spend at least 10 seconds longer on a post if there's a video to watch. Doesn't sound long, does it? But in social media land, where it takes less than a second to scroll through five posts in a newsfeed, 10 seconds is a long time, and Facebook knows it. That's 10 additional seconds where you might click on an ad or be neighbourly on Facebook's land.

Facebook Live is another great option, if you have the courage! With Live you could host a mini webinar on a topic of interest, or, if you have expertise in a particular area – for example medical editing – you could run a live Q&A session.

One thing to bear in mind with Live is that it's broadband-hungry. If your connection and speed are strong, try it.

If going into general population feels like too much of a leap, use one of your smaller groups or invite specific people to the party.

You can go live on your Profile or your Page, but your Page is where you get the organic reach.

- On your Page go to Publishing Tools, Create, Live Video
- On your Profile, click on the Live Video icon in the post window

Optimize your post with audience-centric scheduling

Share posts on your page when most of your followers and fans are online. The posts have more chance of being engaged with and of achieving higher organic reach.

The Insights tab is your friend here. Then select Posts from the menu.

Native blog posts

Now you can stretch your blogging efforts by republishing posts on your Page using Notes. This tool has come a long way since it was first introduced. Give the post a slightly different title so that it's visible two ways in the search engines.

Notes allows us to curate our own content from right within Facebook. That means it's visible to those who might not know of our website, blog, and vlog, or follow us on other social media platforms. It allows colleagues and our potential customers to see what we're creating and to engage with it without leaving the platform.

Rather than seeing it as content duplication, think of it as serving different readers preferences for engaging with your content.

You retain copyright on any content you publish on Facebook. See Section 2 of its Terms of Service.

Facebook groups

Pick two or three that help push you forward (see 'Within-platform focus'). Facebook groups can be superb for problem-solving, information-gathering, content inspiration, knowledge sharing, and networking. Many national editorial societies have dedicated groups. There are also groups dedicated to niche aspects of business such as fiction editing, professional development, science editing, legal editing, and tech tools.

Some editors have created have regular themed threads that help us to be more purposeful.

If you set up your own group, consider assigning posts to Units so that new joiners can easily access discussion threads on topics of interest.

Case study

Sarah Groenendijk's creates a weekly blog post round-up in the Editors' Association of Earth group. Groenendijk starts a new thread every Monday and hashtags it so that older threads are discoverable (#blog). It's a one-stop shop that helps editors see what others have been writing about, and it's a great promo opportunity for the bloggers. Importantly, it's also put Groenendijk front and centre, and is an excellent example of purposeful content curation.

Other steps you can take

Settings

- Verified Pages appear higher in search results. Go to Page, Settings, General, and Page Visibility to verify yours.
- Add a call-to-action button below your Page profile picture.
- Check the Notifications tab in the ribbon at the top of Facebook. It's your shortcut to see who's tagged you and who's engaging with the posts you're engaging with.

Help your audience to love you

- If including links in posts, shorten the URLs using tools such as Ow.ly, Bit.ly or Rebrandly.
- Shorter links are more aesthetically pleasing and take up less space.
- Share the love. If people engage with your posts and share them, reciprocate.

- Don't be embarrassed to ask your Profile friends (those who are in your industry) to like your Page. It's accepted practice. And the more likes your Page has, the bigger your audience reach when you post.
- Don't forget – on your Page it's all about value. The Page is your business's shop front on Facebook so it should look great, be branded (so it's recognizable), be updated regularly, and curate the very best content (yours and others'). Facebook itself urges people to make their posts informative or entertaining. Do one or the other and you're more likely to get attention. And since Facebook's told us this, we know it must be part of the algorithm. When it comes to your Page, 'entertainment' should always be on-brand. If you're worried about whether a post represents you well professionally, save it for selected audiences on your Profile.

For you to do …

Review your social media goals and record in your workbook how you will achieve them on Facebook. Examples could include:

- Chatbot campaign
- Native blogging
- Standard posting
- Uploading video
- Commenting on and sharing key influencers' posts
- Curating themed content threads in Facebook groups

10. How to get Twitter engagement for free

Overview

Twitter's great but it's so darn noisy! However, a lot of my colleagues and potential clients use it, so I do too. It's not the same kind of conversational and networking animal as Facebook but it's a fabulous one-stop shop for industry news and a great way of delivering one's own content quickly to a large number of people. And that's why I still love it.

Basic premise of engagement

Twitter's own analysis of over two million tweets found the following ('What fuels a Tweet's engagement?'):

- Photos/images boost engagement with retweets by 35%.
- Videos boost engagement by 28%.
- Quotes boost engagement with retweets by 19%.
- Including a number bumps up engagement with retweets by 17%.
- Hashtags receive a 16% boost: Don't overdo it so that your post is unreadable. Rather, use hashtags purposefully to align your post with a popular and relevant event or action (e.g. #amediting, #amwriting, #ciep2019).

And in '5 ways to increase your Tweet engagements with emojis', Twitter discusses how emojis draw attention to your posts:

- They act as tiny elevator pitches that let people know what your tweet is bringing to the table. For example, a book review (book emoji); a crime-writing festival (detective emoji); a podcast episode (mic emoji).
- You can use them to show emotion. For example, hearts and smiles are universally understood.

- They can aid navigation by directing the eye to an image or link in the tweet (e.g. arrow emoji; pointing finger emoji).

Using images, gifs, and video in Twitter

Twitter loves images. Twitter users love them too. Remember the research findings:

- Photos/images boost engagement with retweets by 35%
- Videos boost engagement by 28%

That stream of text is an eyesore and it's almost impossible to make sense of what's on offer without visual clues. With this in mind, when you post to Twitter, think about how you might help your audience make sense of the value you're offering.

- Can you use visuals to make them feel something (happy, for example)?
- Can you use visuals to prove you're going to help them?

Visuals can be used entertain (gif), inform (thumbnail), increase recognizability (branding), and engage (video), all of which makes us stand out among all the noise.

Emotional attention: The juggling snowman gif

Here are some of the screenshots I used to create a seasonal gif for my Twitter followers. The book theme keeps things on-brand, but the primary aim is to bring a smile to my audience's faces.

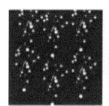   

To create a gif, create images in Canva and upload to a tool such Gifmaker.me or Giphy. Then add to your tweet using the photo button.

Informational attention: What's on offer

Here's are two images. The first tells my indie-author followers why they should click on the link I've tweeted about a blog post on writing great chapter endings. Note that the images are branded – I use consistent formatting that's recognizable.

The second from Denise Cowle explains that the link with lead through to writing guidance.

Video

You can either upload existing short videos to Twitter or go live on your smart phone or tablet using Twitter's native video broadcasting tool, Periscope. While gifs and thumbnail images are uploaded by many Twitter users, video is still an underused engagement tool and therefore an opportunity to stand out.

Twitter lists

Twitter lists make Twitter manageable, especially if you're the kind of person who likes to follow back most of the people who follow you. To create and add someone to a list, click on their profile, head up to the three dots on the right-hand side of the ribbon below the banner, select 'Add/ Remove from Lists', then select either 'Create List' or check the box for an existing list.

Lists take you away from the main feed and into something that's focused, which is great for purposeful engagement. The feed is much smaller and – unless you're celebrity-popular – perfectly capable of being attended to in its entirety!

Threads and Moments

Threads support users who want to publish stories that exceed the 280-character limit. Tweetstorms are not new but this feature enables users to connect up to 25 individual tweets in a thread in one hit. You can edit any tweet in the thread while you're in draft form, and add video or gifs, just as you might with a normal tweet.

To create a thread, type your first tweet. When you're done, press the + button to create and attach a new tweet.

So how might we use this? I think it could be Twitter's alternative to LinkedIn and Facebook's native blogging platforms, but slimmed down. Try posting the following:

- Summaries of core themes in blog posts
- To promote a series of related blogs, vlogs or podcasts
- Modules in training courses
- Mini reviews of software, books and course
- Summaries of speaking engagements or other events
- Lists of useful editorial tools and resources

Visit the thread for my 'Countdown to Christmas Catchup' advent calendar to see an example of how I linked 12 tweets to allow people to catch up on the gifts they'd missed. I found the thread easy to build, far more so than Moments.

An alternative is to create a Moment, though they're fiddlier than Threads because you have to locate and collate existing tweets, which can be cumbersome if you're a heavy Twitter user.

John Espirian's '10 Writing Tips' is another example. The same principle applies in terms of connection, but the tweets are individually posted and curated later. To build your curated tweet thread, go to the tweet you want to add, click on the chevron in the top-right-hand corner, and select Add to New Moment. You'll be directed to give your Moment a title. Continue adding new tweets to the Moment until you're done. Then add a picture and publish.

Other steps you can take

Implement the following tweaks to improve your users' experience. Click on your profile picture in the top right-hand corner. From the dropdown menu select Settings and Privacy.

Privacy and location

- Check Tweet with a location if you want to ground yourself a little.
- Check the Discoverability options if you want to help people find you other than by name.
- Check the Direct Messages box if you want to make yourself contactable via DM by anyone.

Mobile

- Add your mobile phone number if you'd like to be able to receive text messages from Twitter.

Accessibility

- Check the Image descriptions box to give visually impaired users a better experience of your tweets.
- On your desktop or laptop, select Tweet, click on the image icon in the bottom left-hand corner of the tweet window, and select your image from your computer. When it's uploaded, click on it. A dialogue box will open into which you can type your text.
- For full instructions on how to add alt-text or a voice-over that describes your images on a range of devices, read 'How to make images accessible for people'.

Add business-support features

- Go to: https://business.twitter.com/i/settings/support
- Check the Receive Direct Messages from anyone box
- Check the Show that my account provides support box

- Tweak your support hours
- Search for your invisible mentions
- Search for hidden mentions of yourself so you can increase your engagement: e.g. "louise Harnby" - from:louiseharnby -@louiseharnby

Respect the algorithms

- Ensure your profile is complete, branded, and that your key links are included (e.g. website, blog, or resource hub).
- If someone retweets you, retweet that retweet! It boosts engagement.
- Regularly reschedule top-performing tweets. Twitter is so noisy that it's easier to miss a tweet than see it.

Use analytics

- Twitter Analytics is worth a gander to give you an indication of whether your audience is changing and which tweets have garnered the greatest engagement.

Use the tools

- TwitterChats are great for this platform's version of targeted online business networking (e.g. #EFAchat, #ACESchat). They're quickfire and you're limited to by the usual character count, so you need to be succinct.
- Create a poll to get a glimpse of people's views on a topic. These can be handy for blog-post research.
- You can embed tweets in your blog posts: click the chevron in the top-right corner of a tweet, select Embed Tweet, and copy the code and paste it into your website using the embed-code tool.

Help your audience to love you

- Share the love. Respond and reciprocate.
- If including links in comments, shorten the URLs.
- Focus on value. Posts that help make your colleagues' and clients' lives easier are more likely to create purposeful engagement that leads to business opportunities.

For you to do ...

Review your social media goals and record in your workbook how you will achieve them on Twitter. Examples could include:

- Using gifs
- Mini-blogging via Threads
- Uploading video
- Commenting on and sharing key influencers' tweets

11. How to get LinkedIn engagement for free

Overview

LinkedIn has changed. It's far less formal these days – the LinkedIn community no longer restricts its conversations to groups; people are asking questions, posting opinion, commenting, and even creating native video in the main feed.

It's still a different animal from Facebook and Twitter in terms of ease of engagement but for editorial professionals who are targeting businesses, it's THE place to engage.

My colleague John Espirian offers technical writing and consulting services to the business community. LinkedIn is his number-one social media platform. He's done extensive research into how to make LinkedIn work; I've summarized his findings here but head to his website if you want to dominate this platform in your field.

Write text-only posts

Yup, this is the complete opposite of Twitter and Facebook! To get the biggest rewards from LinkedIn, post your images and links in the first comment instead. The meat of your main post is text only.

Remember the story about neighbourliness on Facebook Street and Website Street, and the money issue? The same principle is at work here – LinkedIn rewards you for keeping people on its own land so that it can sell to users.

My LinkedIn posts usually receive between 40 and 90 views. That's because this isn't my primary platform and I tend to break all the algorithm rules – not much text, an embedded link to my blog, and an image. But I've tested John's theory by taking a post that had achieved 84 views and returning to LinkedIn with the same information, but this time playing the algorithm game. I summarized the content of the blog article, and added the title and link to my website in the first comment. Just switching around my approach increased my audience reach tenfold. If you're serious about using LinkedIn purposefully, follow the text-only approach. It works.

Ask questions

If you want to see LinkedIn question-posing in action, look at what Janet Murray does. Murray asks questions most days, from 'What was your first car?' to 'What's your most embarrassing social media gaffe?'.

This mix of personal and professional engagement is text-only, drives engagement (because questions require answers), and generates content for her PR podcast. And because, over time, she's generated an engaged following in the fields of marketing, communications and public relations, she gets a lot of engagement, and a big fat boost from LinkedIn whenever she posts.

She plays the algorithm game and she always plays nice. And here's where the same rules apply as on other networks ... she's polite and professional – her posts don't get reported – and she responds. That makes people want to engage with her.

She also frequently tags people at the bottom of her posts – it's her way of tapping someone on the shoulder and asking for a response (it's no different to the tagging we do on Facebook or Twitter).

Native blog posts

You can post blog articles directly on LinkedIn (via Publishing, LinkedIn's blogging platform). Espirian recommends posting the content on your own website first. That way, in Google's eyes, the authority for the post lies with your primary business platform.

Seven days later, repurpose the post for LinkedIn. Tweak the title so that it's findable in the search engines for two different search queries.

You retain copyright on any content you publish on LinkedIn. See Section 3.1 of its User Agreement.

Other steps you can take

Search for hidden mentions

Search for hidden mentions of yourself in the mobile app to increase your engagement:

- Search for your name.
- Tap the Content tab, then Filters, 1st connections, Latest, Done.

Engage with yourself

- Share your shares.
- Like your own posts.
- Embed your LinkedIn content in your blog posts: click the ellipsis in the top-right corner of a post, Select Embed this post, then Copy code. Paste the code into your website using the embed-code tool.

Personalize your invitations

- John Espirian estimates that only about 10% of invitations are customized so this is an easy way to stand out.

Settings

- Update your privacy settings so that 'Everyone' can see your updates and follow you.

Respect the algorithms

- Upload video natively rather than embedding links to videos hosted elsewhere.
- Ensure your profile is complete. This is particularly important for LinkedIn. We know so because it often reminds us when we need to add something. Even if it feels like a bore to add in this seemingly uninteresting

information, do so – LinkedIn's algorithm thinks it matters!

Help your audience to love you

- Share the love. Respond to comments on your own posts and reciprocate.
- Focus on value. As always, posts that help make your colleagues' and clients' lives easier are more likely to create purposeful engagement that leads to business opportunities.
- If including links in comments, shorten the URLs.

For you to do ...

Review your social media goals and record in your workbook how you will achieve them on LinkedIn. Examples could include:

- Text-only posts
- Native blogging
- Standard posting
- Posing questions
- Uploading video
- Commenting on and sharing key influencers' posts

12. Using video

Overview

Video is a great way of showing the real you on social media. I've had lots of people tell me they enjoyed hearing my voice and seeing me in motion. That's because many of us are 'friends' with hundreds, perhaps thousands of colleagues from all over the world, and yet we only get to meet a small percentage in person. Video's like a halfway house.

We're back to emotion. When you put your face, your voice, your smile on social media you evoke emotion in people. And emotion is more likely to drive engagement and strengthen your presence; it makes your marketing efforts stickier, more memorable.

If you've scrolled through pages of text on one of your social media feeds and come across a video of one of your colleagues or clients, it piques your curiosity because text-based posts are still the most common way of communicating on social media and anything different stands out.

Of course, for purposeful business engagement, the videos should be on-brand and on point. Even if you're nervous about using video, bear in mind that videos encourage engagement and play to the algorithms' preferences. You're likely to get better reach if you can embrace it.

Video is also important because not all our colleagues and clients want to consume our content in the same way. When we introduce video into the mix, we're offering people a choice of how to engage with what we say on social media.

Social media options

You can upload a pre-recorded video from your preferred device (e.g. laptop, tablet, smart phone or desktop) or, if you're feeling brave, go live. Twitter, LinkedIn, Facebook and YouTube allow you to do both. Smart phones do a great job of recording.

Video is chunky in terms of file size, and uploading to anywhere, especially Facebook, can take an age, especially if your broadband is slow. I recommend Handbrake, a free compression tool, to speed things up.

If you're going live, take into account your broadband speed – if yours is slow it can cause lagging at best and failure at worst.

How to use video

Video is a great way of complementing your text posts on social media. Your videos don't have to be long. Depending on your intention they could be shorties of only 20–30 seconds. Here are a few ideas for you to try:

- Announce an event that you're speaking at
- Record an introduction to a blog post
- Announce a forthcoming conference at which you're speaking
- Tell people about a blog, vlog or podcast episode you've recently published
- Create a vlog version of your blog content
- Thank a colleague or potential client for retweeting you
- Say hello to a new follower
- Congratulate someone on a piece of great content they've created
- Send your followers your seasonal best wishes
- Launch a new product or service
- Embed a tutorial

Case study 1: Facebook

Here's how I've used video on Facebook. The following screenshots depict two videos: the one on the left is 4-minute summary of a blog post about editing erotica; on the right is Crystal Pikko Watanabe's charming and informative Page-based services video in which she takes potential clients through the steps of how to make a booking, all the while emphasizing the importance of a sample evaluation and a good-fit relationship.

Case study 2: Twitter

Pete Gartland, one half of pro marketers Andrew and Pete, used Twitter video (recorded live on Periscope) to thank me for sharing some of the A&P content and to ask me about my own video marketing journey. I wasn't yet a client, but Pete used video to engage with me personally, and I still remember what an impact it made on me – no one outside of my network had ever made that kind of one-to-one effort on a social media platform before.

It's important to understand what Pete was doing here. He wasn't trying to be my new best friend. Rather, his intention was to use social media to arouse emotion in me, such that if I decided to commission pro marketing training, Andrew and Pete would be top of mind.

And it worked (in association with their great content) – I was looking for pro training. I did my research and considered several options to develop my content marketing skills, but no one came close. I signed up a month later.

Be purposeful

The golden rule with video is to be purposeful. Social media is noisy and no one wants to feel that their time is being wasted or that they've learned nothing but what the insides of your nostrils look like.

So be clear on what your intention is – whether that's explaining, announcing or teaching something, asking a question, or directing someone somewhere. The best social media videos make the viewer feel something, e.g. happy, grateful, informed.

It's about emotion – and from that comes stickiness and memorability.

Why not try using video to advertise your services or blog posts? You don't have to go face-to-camera. You could use images and creates gifs from the stills with Gifmaker and Giphy allow you to create videos as well as gifs from your still images.

My favourite, favourite gadget for creating smashing videos from stills is MoShow (currently only available for IOS devices).

Go native

Remember the algorithms? Social media wants you to stay on its land so the most effective videos will be those that are uploaded onto the platform rather than accessed via links to a third-party website like YouTube or Vimeo.

Subtitles/captions

A whopping 85% of videos are played with the sound off! Creating subtitles/captions for your social media videos is therefore a good idea. Creating captions respects people who are hard-of-hearing and those with different preferences.

You can create subtitles for free in YouTube or pay a small fee in Rev.com.

If you're uploading a video to social media that's also hosted on YouTube, you can create the captions (or edit the automatic ones) directly in YouTube and download the files for free. These can then be uploaded to the social media version of your video.

Creating and downloading caption files in YouTube

Upload your video to YouTube. Go to Creator Studio. Your videos will appear in a column. To add subtitles, select Edit, then Subtitles/CC. Edit the English (Automatic) version and save. YouTube will save your edited subtitles as English. To download the captions file, go to YouTube:

- Click on your video title
- Select Subtitles/CC
- Select your newly created edited captions

- Go to Actions and select .srt. Your captions file will download

Attaching captions to native Facebook videos

Before you do anything else, change the file name from captions.srt to [title].en_US.srt. You won't be able to upload if you don't carry out this step. Upload your video into Facebook (just as you'd attach a photo or image). Then go to your Page and look in the left-hand navigation bar. Select Videos, then click on the title of the video you wish to upload captions to.

- Open the dropdown menu from the ellipsis and select Edit Post.
- Select Captions, then Upload SRT File. Choose your renamed file and save.

Attaching captions to native Twitter and LinkedIn videos

Twitter and LinkedIn are a little behind Facebook. Here are three options for you try based on what software you have or prefer:

- If you're on an Apple phone, record the video with an app that adds live captions, e.g. Apple Clips.
- Import the .srt file into a video-creator app then export the video with burned-in captions.
- Burn in the captions to an existing video using Handbrake.

For you to do …

Review your social media goals and record ideas in your workbook about how you could incorporate video into the mix. Examples could include:

- Shortie videos that say hello or thank you
- Service videos that promote your business
- Tutorials that help clients or colleagues solve problems

Consider which tools you will use for creation and curation. Examples might include:

- YouTube and Vimeo
- MoShow, Lumen5 and Raw Shorts
- Handbrake
- Smart phone, tablet, desktop

13: Using images

Overview

Images add interest and make social media posts more engaging (though see the LinkedIn chapter for caution). If you're posting links to blog content, it's likely that an image will be pulled from the post automatically. Otherwise, create one specifically for social media in something like Canva.

For purposeful business use, keep the images on point so that they tell clients and colleagues what you do. Consider also augmenting your social media posts with pictures that announce, inform, and make your posts stand out.

Canva

Canva is simply the niftiest free online graphic-design tool for non-designers! There are many templates to choose from, all with preset sizes recommended by the core social media platforms. I recommend using Canva to create the following in social media:

- Social media banners
- Images for posts
- Images for gif creation

Canva offers an onboard selection of free images, but the free version also allows you to upload your own. Also try Unsplash and Pixabay.

Compressing images

Images can be chunky and increase page-load times. There are hundreds of image compressors available for free online. I recommend TinyPNG. It works on jpegs and pngs. It's quick, rarely glitches, and slims images to a fraction of their former size with minimal loss of quality.

Gifs

Gifs are teeny-weeny videos – a collection of images on steroids! They're a fun and alternative way to draw your audience's attention to your social media posts and evoke emotion. You can use digital photographs, stills from your videos, or create images in Canva.

Once you have your images, upload the media to a gif creator. I recommend Gifmaker.me and Giphy. There are many free online alternatives.

Here are some ideas for how to use gifs purposefully:

- To greet people
- To thank people for sharing a post
- As a mini video to draw attention to your post
- To engage seasonally with your social media followers and make them smile

Branding your images and gifs

Don't forget to brand your images so that your posts are recognizable. Consider your brand colours, your logo, the tone or feel of the image, and your face.

For you to do

Review your social media goals and make a note in your workbook of how you could incorporate images into the mix to make your posts more engaging. Examples could include:

- Informational thumbnails
- Gifs
- Professional headshots and logos
- Industry-related quotes

Consider which tools you will use for creation. Examples might include:

- Canva
- TinyPNG

14. Branding your social media channels

Branding your social media channels consistently is essential. Your colleagues have thousands of fellow editors on social media platforms and no time to seek them out individually. Branding makes life easier for them and you.

A strong brand identity is recognizable. Make an impact in one place and you won't have to work as hard in others; trust, credibility and authority are already established.

Headshots

Some of you may have commissioned professional headshots; others will have asked a friend to take a picture with a half-decent camera. Whatever route you've chosen, if you're using social media for professional purposes your images should reflect that and be consistent across all platforms (recognizability). Here are some guidelines:

- No silly wigs – unless you're selling silly wigs rather than editorial/publishing services.
- No blurry stuff – if your headshot looks sloppy, what does that say about your work?
- Your partner, your best mate, or your kids shouldn't be in the picture either – not on professional profiles. Stick the buddy pictures on your personal Facebook Profile to your heart's content, but those are not what should be showing up on your Facebook Page, your LinkedIn banner, or your Twitter profile.

Images are worth a thousand words, or so they say. A great headshot is like turning up to an interview dressed appropriately. A poor one is like turning up with your breakfast on your shirt. Good headshots will be usable for years so it's worth investing a little time to get them right.

Brand colours

Do you know your brand colours? If you don't, you should! That way you can ensure your social media images match your website, business cards, and other promo materials. Again, it's all about consistency.

- If you want lighter colours, then change your brand colours' opacity, not the colours themselves.
- Use a hex–RGB converter to keep your brand colours standard across different platforms (e.g. Twitter uses hex colours. So does my website host, Weebly. Microsoft Office uses RGB). I recommend Yellowpipe because it converts both ways – from hex to RBG and RGB to hex.

Logo

Not everyone has a logo – I got one in 2017 after over a decade in business. I managed perfectly well without it for years; it was a treat to myself, the icing on my branding cake! For me, it's my brand identity in a nutshell.

If you have a logo, use it on your social media images and banners. It's yet another opportunity to reinforce your recognizable brand. And there's nothing more individual!

Handles

Consistency across channels can be tricky as some platforms restrict the number of characters and whether you can use special characters. Do the best you can in order to be findable and recognizable. Here's an example of best practice:

- Business: Lisa Poisso. Book Editor. Writing Coach
- Facebook Page: Lisa Poisso – Book Editor & Writing Coach
- Twitter handle: @LisaPoisso
- LinkedIn name: Lisa Poisso
- Pinterest: LisaPoissoEditor

Images and banners

Use your brand colours, logo, and headshot to put your own individual stamps on the images you use on social media. Think about the following:

- Social media profile banners
- Images you upload or share (e.g. images used in blog posts; cover images of PDF resources such as checklists or booklets)

Some platforms (such as Twitter) will let you customize the colours of links and headers. Knowing your brand colours will ensure you can match these to your images and create a strong, recognizable impact.

For you to do ...

Review your emotion-arousal goals and think about your brand identity in light of these:

- Does your tone and the content you're delivering arouse the emotions you're aiming for?
- Are you recognizable and trusted across your core platforms?
- Are your social media profiles complete and error-free?
- Are you handles consistent and recognizable?
- Are your social media images branded consistently?
- Do you know your brand colours?

Use the strategy workbook to record which elements of branding are already in place, what needs tweaking, and what needs implementing from scratch.

15. Management, scheduling, and analytics

Time can feel like a leaky bucket when it comes to social media. And the larger one's network, the heavier the spillage. Here are some tips to help you keep the mop at bay.

Time and efficiency

Find a rhythm that gets you into your flow and then stick to it. Here are some tips for managing your time effectively. It's one way, not the way. I offer it as an example, nothing more.

30-minute coffee break

Dedicate specific time each day to the management of your purposeful social media activity. I like to grab myself a coffee around 9.30 a.m. (post-dog walk and pre-editing at 10 a.m.). During that half hour I check Feedly and do the bulk of my colleagues' content sharing. Then I turn to my Twitter, LinkedIn, and Facebook notifications to see whether I need to respond to someone's engagement with me.

Finally, I look at Buffer to make sure that all my content for the day is scheduled (or rescheduled).

The evening's social networking

In the evenings, I multitask. That means doubling up on watching the evening news on TV and checking in on Facebook group conversations. If it's in my own group, that's a priority. If it's in another group and I'm tagged, that's a priority too. If I'm not, my input will be determined by how much I have to offer that's new, what else is going on at home, and how strongly I feel about an issue.

If you fancy trying this model, but worry you'll overstep the mark timewise, set an alarm on your phone to remind you that you're near the rabbit hole.

Leaving groups and deleting apps

If you're concerned that being a member of a social media group almost compels you to engage despite your best intentions to cut back, consider leaving it. Evaluate the impact after 30 days. Are there consequences?

- Has your work stream suffered?
- Have you received negative feedback from colleagues?
- Has the reduced interaction left you feeling isolated?

If the answer to the above questions is no, you've learned something valuable – your business won't collapse with this one decision.

My colleague John Espirian drastically cut back on his Facebook engagement after just such an exercise. LinkedIn is his primary platform and he elected to dedicate himself to that and Twitter with no deleterious results. In fact, the impact has been positive because he now concentrates his time in the space that gives him the best return on investment.

The fact is this – everyone in your network is as busy as you, and the larger editorial social media groups have enough members to ensure that one person's cutting back on engagement is not going to have a major impact.

You might also consider deleting apps on your phone and tablet so that you're forced to limit your social media engagement to specific devices, located in specific places (e.g. your office), and accessible only during specific times of the day.

Tracking others' content

To track what your network is up to, and what you might want to share (or re-share), I recommend the following:

- Feedly: This is great for keeping an eye on what colleagues and clients are up to. Set up feeds for different types of content (e.g. I have one called Editing). When you learn of a blog you're interested in, add it to your dedicated feed. Then drop in every few days and see who's published what. Once you've found content of interest in Feedly, share it on social media. Sharing can be done direct from the feed and by clicking through to the original content. An advantage of using something like Feedly is that it reduces the need for blog-subscription and mailing-list signup, both of which can turn your email inbox into yet another rabbit hole.

- Twitter lists: These are lifesavers. I have lists for editorial folk, training, marketing, self-publishing, and authors. Those are where I head when I'm ready to engage, not the hell that is my Twitter Home feed!
- Facebook: Facebook's a little tricky when it comes to deciding what content it's going to show us first, but we can only do our best. Head for the Home button on the Facebook ribbon and use it to check the latest news. Will you catch everything? Not a chance, but you're being purposeful so you have to work with what you've got!
- LinkedIn: Again, it's the Home button that you need to head for if you want to see what's going on in your network.

Scheduling

If you're producing regular content and making it visible via your core social media platforms, you're going to need a scheduler. The beauty of a scheduler is that it allows you to manage the posting of one piece of content over several different social media platforms at the same time.

There are lots to choose from: Buffer, Hootsuite, SmarterQueue Recurpost, Jarvis … Some are free; others have premium versions with higher functionality. Some monitor what your network's up to, which makes the dashboard more crowded, naturally.

I use Buffer but I recommend trying several so you can evaluate what works for you.

Reposting content on social media

To maximize engagement, you should be posting regularly so that you build a reputation as an editorial professional who is consistently engaged. So how often should you reschedule content? It depends on the platform, where your audience is hanging out, and what's performing well.

Consider the noise levels and pace – the greater the traffic levels and the higher the speed at which posts appear, the more likely your post is to be buried and the more you can reschedule without frustrating your audience.

Over-posting can frustrate followers. Under-posting leads to invisibility. Balance noise and pace in a way that respects this.

- Twitter: It's noisy, with new tweets appearing every second. Chances are that most people whom you'd like to see your tweets will miss them.
- Facebook: It's big for editorial professionals, but intimate too, with a slower post pace.
- LinkedIn: I post updates about new content on LinkedIn once a day.

Evaluating

Evaluating what's popular is key to purposeful social media engagement. Most social media platforms and most free schedulers offer analytics but they're basic.

The free version of BuzzSumo shows you the top five pieces of content on your website in the past year and what engagement took place on some social media platforms. It is just a snapshot, so broader analytics shouldn't be ignored, but it's handy for giving one a sense of which platforms generate the best engagement.

My two preferred analytics tools – Google Analytics and StatCounter – are much better at giving me a broad picture of what people are looking at on my website and where those views have come from (e.g. Facebook, Twitter, or LinkedIn).

Go to your Google Analytics dashboard. Select Acquisition then Channels from the left-hand menu. In the data window that opens, click on Social. That shows you exactly which social media platforms are generating the highest engagement. GA is brilliant at helping us make decisions that are based on data rather than instinct. I recommend Andy Crestodina's blog at Orbit Media for straightforward advice on how to use Google Analytics purposefully.

For you to do …

Use your strategy workbook to record when and how you will engage with each of your core platforms as part of your business-growth strategy:

- Create a schedule that fits the flow of your day.
- Consider the tools you'll use to schedule posts.
- Think about the pace and noise of each platform to manage frequency.
- Select analytics programs that will guide you with data.
- Set up tracking tools to make social media feeds manageable.

16. Does it work?

Social media isn't the answer to everything. It needs careful management if we're to make it work for our businesses. Overindulgence sucks time out of our working day and makes us less productive.

Still, ignoring it is a mistake. Taken as a whole, social media offers editors the single biggest global platform on which to network, build awareness of our brands, advertise our products and services, seek assistance, and message each other ... and without a penny changing hands.

It's versatile too. We're not limited to words. We can also post pictures, upload files, embed audio and video, create polls, and run competitions. We can join big groups and small ones, and even create our own and fill them with only those we choose to. That means even the introverted among us can find a suitable space in the social ether.

Will you get work as a result of regular, purposeful social media engagement? Yes, though it won't necessarily come direct. One author or publisher might search a platform for an editor; another might find you via the content you've shared on social media; another might discover you because they're watching a discussion you're contributing too; and another might use social media to verify that you are who you say you are. One thing's for sure – if you're not using social media for business, you're decreasing your visibility options.

Let's finish with this sage reminder from Grant Leboff (*Sticky Marketing*, p. 123):

> 'Businesses do need to utilize social networking sites, because whether it is Facebook, LinkedIn Twitter or one of the many others, inevitably their customers will be on them.'

Appendix 1: Resources

10 Writing Tips: John Espirian:
  https://mobile.twitter.com/i/events/839077665810300928
Bit.ly: URL shortener (useful analytics included): https://app.bitly.com
Buffer: Social media scheduler: https://buffer.com
BuzzSumo: Social media engagement and content analysis tool:
  https://app.buzzsumo.com
Canva Copy Special: Free downloadable templates from Andrew and
  Pete: https://www.andrewandpete.com/how-to-create-social-media-
  graphics
Canva: Graphic-design tool for non-designers: http://www.canva.com
Chatbot comments campaign walkthrough: How to Market Your Book
  and Build Your Author Platform Using a Chatbot: Part 1 – Facebook
  Comments: https://www.louiseharnbyproofreader.com/blog/how-to-
  market-your-book-and-build-your-author-platform-using-a-chatbot-
  part-1-facebook-comments
Countdown to Christmas Catch-up:
  https://twitter.com/LouiseHarnby/status/940928459576152064
Crestodina, Andy: *Content Chemistry,* 5th edition, Orbit Media Studios,
  2019
Editorial societies: Global list of professional associations:
  https://www.louiseharnbyproofreader.com/editing--proofreading-
  societies.html
Editors' Association of Earth: Facebook group:
  https://www.facebook.com/groups/EditorsofEarth
Feedly: Content-curation tool: https://feedly.com
Gifmaker.me: Gif-creation tool: http://gifmaker.me
Giphy: Gif-creation tool: https://giphy.com
Google Analytics: http://www.google.com/analytics
Handbrake: Free video compression tool: https://handbrake.fr
Leboff, Grant: *Sticky Marketing*, Kogan Page, 2011
MailChimp: Mailing-list and blog-subscription management tool:
  https://mailchimp.com
ManyChat: Chatbot creation tool and campaign generator:
  https://manychat.com

MoShow: Slideshow movie-maker app available from iTunes: https://moshowapp.com

Orbit Media Studios blog: https://www.orbitmedia.com/blog

Ow.ly: URL shortener: http://ow.ly/url/shorten-url

Pinterest board example 1: Louise's Editing, Proofreading & Writing Library: https://www.pinterest.co.uk/louiseharnbyeditor/louises-editing-proofreading-writing-library

Pinterest board example 2: Northern Editorial: Writing and Editing: https://www.pinterest.co.uk/northerneditor/writing-and-editing

Pinterest Save Button: Chrome extension: https://chrome.google.com/webstore/search/pinterest

Raw Shorts: Drag-and-drop explainer video-animation tool (free and low-cost premium options): https://www.rawshorts.com

Rebrandly: Link shortener: http://www.rebrandly.com

Recurpost: Social media scheduler: https://recurpost.com

Rev: Captions, transcription and translation service (not free but low cost; there's a free and self-editable service in YouTube): https://www.rev.com

Shareaholic: Social media sharing buttons: https://shareaholic.com

StatCounter: Analytics tool: http://statcounter.com

TinyPNG: Compresses chunky PNGs and JPGs with minimal loss of quality: https://tinypng.com

Tutorial from Andrew and Pete: How to Create Social Media Graphics: https://www.andrewandpete.com/how-to-create-social-media-graphics

Tutorial from Jessica Tangelder on how to add captions into a video using Handbrake: How to Use Handbrake to Burn SRT Files in Your MP4/MOV Files: https://www.youtube.com/watch?v=ycVpbXDJswk

Tutorial from Mark Orr of Pocket Video School: Increase Video Upload Speed – Handbrake Tutorial: https://www.youtube.com/watch?v=dkLIqmr9zaE&t=286s.

Tutorial: How to Make Images Accessible for People: https://help.twitter.com/en/using-twitter/picture-descriptions

Twitter: 5 Ways to Increase Your Tweet Engagements with Emojis: https://business.twitter.com/en/blog/5-ways-to-increase-your-tweet-engagements-with-emojis.html

Twitter: What Fuels a Tweet's Engagement?:
   https://blog.twitter.com/official/en_us/a/2014/what-fuels-a-tweets-
   engagement.html
Unsplash: Royalty-free images: https://unsplash.com
Yellowpipe: Brand-colour converter (hex and RGB):
   http://www.yellowpipe.com/yis/tools/hex-to-rgb/color-converter.php
YouTube channel example 1: Louise Harnby: Fiction Editor &
   Proofreader
   http://www.youtube.com/c/LouiseHarnbyProofreaderCopyeditor
YouTube channel example 2: John Espirian (Technical Writer &
   Editor): https://www.youtube.com/user/communus

Appendix 2: How to do social media badly

No matter how social it seems, social media is not the same as chatting with your best friend. If you *do* want to make a spectacular mess of your social media marketing strategy, try this lot!

1. When using social media as a delivery tool, focus on others' content at the expense of your own. You're really generous and your colleagues are grateful; shame they can't reciprocate.
2. Or do the opposite – ignore others. By not reciprocating the effort others have made, you'll build a rep for being selfish. Way to go!
3. Always ask for more than you give. The greedier you are, the harder you'll fail. Woo hoo!
4. Moan about how much time you don't have – that way people will sympathize with the fact that you've been denied the magic pill that some of us take to make a twenty-fifth hour available for social media marketing. Life's so unfair.
5. Moaning is bad so do it often. Moaners don't get referrals because, well, they're moaners and boring. When we moan, it's all about us. Moaning is a sure-fire way to generate no engagement, no trust, and no leads.
6. Ask for advice, then when you get it, say none of it's possible to implement because … (see 4. Moaning). That way, people will come to understand that you simply want them to hand over your client list.
7. If you disagree with someone on social media, make it clear that the other person is just wrong, wrong, wrong. Don't let it go; really pile in on them. That way they'll feel unwelcome.
8. Pointing out spelling and grammar errors is the best disengagement tool in our profession! Humiliation is the name of the game.

9. Feed trolls – engage and loudly as you can. They love it and will drag you to the ground for a thoroughly mucky wrestle. By the time you're done, your confidence will be in tatters and you'll be so distracted you'll make mistakes in your editing work.

10. Automate as much as you can. Especially on Twitter. People get really annoyed by automated direct messages so it's a great way of creating disengagement.

11. Don't build relationships; just get straight to the hard sell. 'Anyone got any work? I don't have time to find my own clients because …' (see 4. Moaning).

12. Discuss your clients' work on social media, e.g. Facebook groups. Ideally, you should mock their errors. You might think those groups are closed and private, but if there are 2.5K members, lots of your colleagues will see how comfortable you are breaching confidentiality in a closed but public space. And if you're really lucky, word will get back to your client. Sure, their mistakes are what give us jobs, but so what? There's nothing like a bit of online head-desking to trash trust!

13. Add your colleagues to social media discussion groups without asking them first. They already struggle to manage their own purposeful social media engagement. When you start making decisions for them – because it suits you – you kick them into the rabbit hole they're trying so hard to stay out of.

14. Add social media buttons to the top of your website so they're front and centre. That way, people can leave your site as quickly as possible, which is fantastic after all the hard work you've done to get them to visit in the first place.

Printed in Great Britain
by Amazon

59492192R00045